CW01309813

Tim J Francis © 2024   www.timjfrancis.com

PUMPKINWEENIE

For Sale

BY
TIM J FRANCIS

John Pulp, the Pumpkin, was the last in the Bumpkin Farm field.
Halloween had come and gone, now John Pulp was just one.
"Hi Pumpkinweenie," said a mouse passing by.
"Hi, why do you call me Pumpkinweenie?
 I'm John Pulp, a scary pumpkin, that's me."
"You're unscary, unwanted and so, not sold."
"The only thing left for you
is the Pumpkin Smasher!
Don't try being bold.
Go."

"There's no such thing as a Pumpkin Smasher.
I'll wait.
I really want to find a family.
Someone will pick me." said John Pulp hopefully.

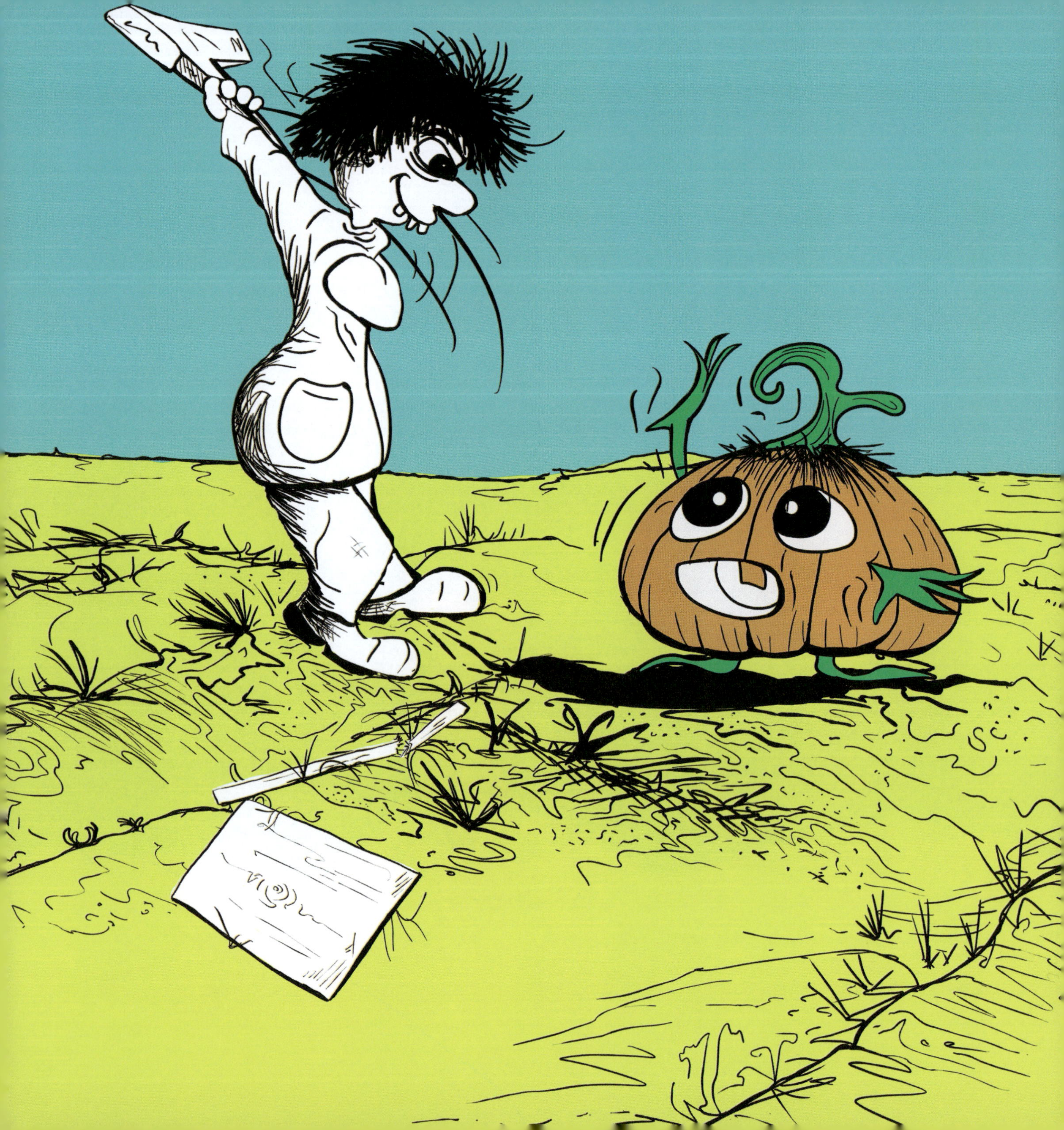

Here came the Pumpkin Smasher swinging an axe.

"One smash with my axe and you'll be dashed!" said the Pumpkin Smasher.

As the axe was about to go crash…
John Pulp leapt and then ran off in a dash.

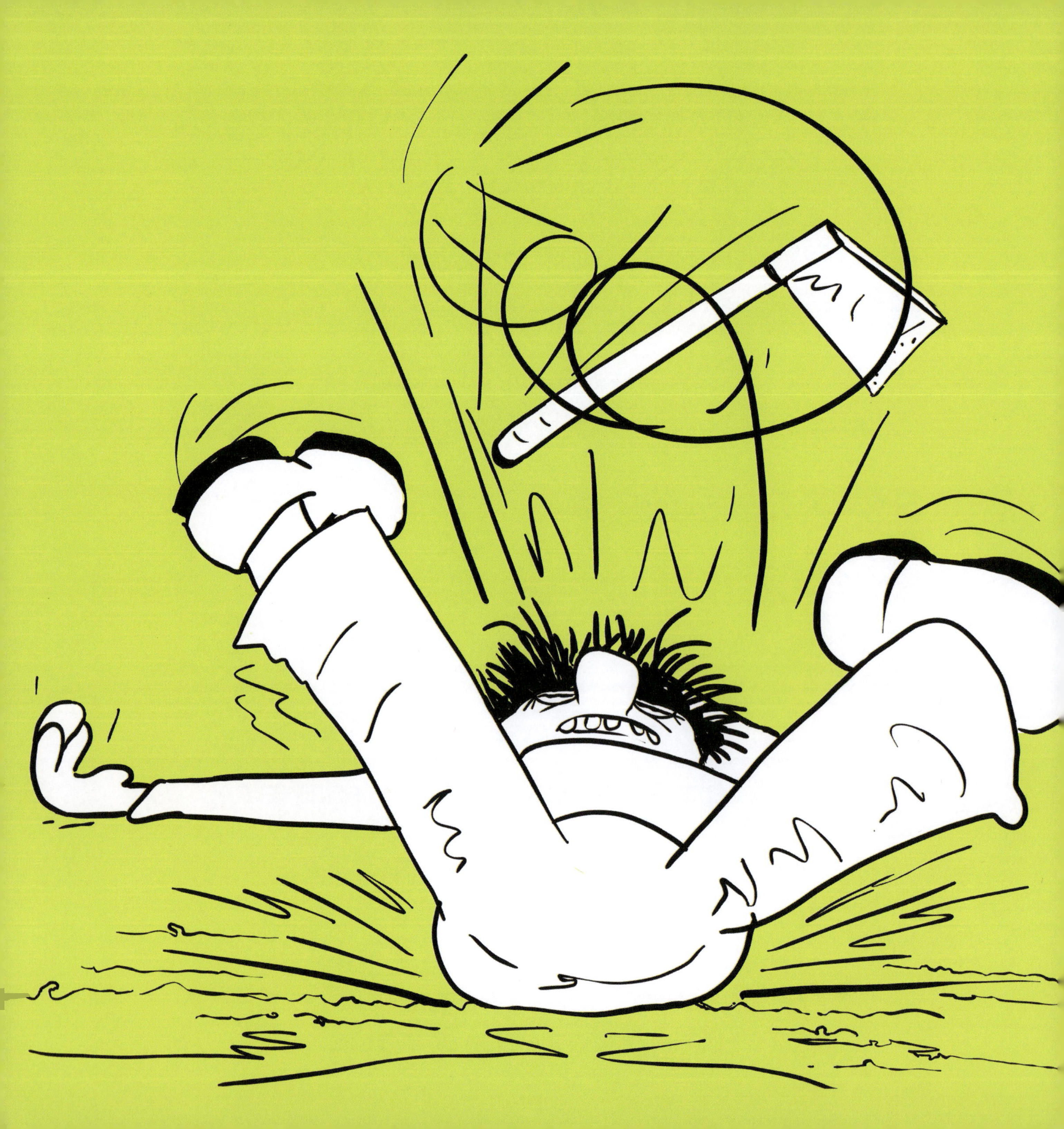

Before a smashing
John Pulp turned and went dashing,
And the Pumpkin Smasher, with a swing and a hiss, missed.

Chasing and smashing,
crashing through the woods,
came the Pumpkin Smasher.
He was getting close,
closer than close.

"Don't smash me!" said John Pulp,
"I just want to be friends."
"A friend? A friend? No, this is your end."
said the Pumpkin Smasher.
So John Pulp ran on.

"You can't get away!" screamed the Pumpkin Smasher from somewhere near.
"Maybe I can hide inside here." said John Pulp, finding a hollowed log.
He was nearly in tears.

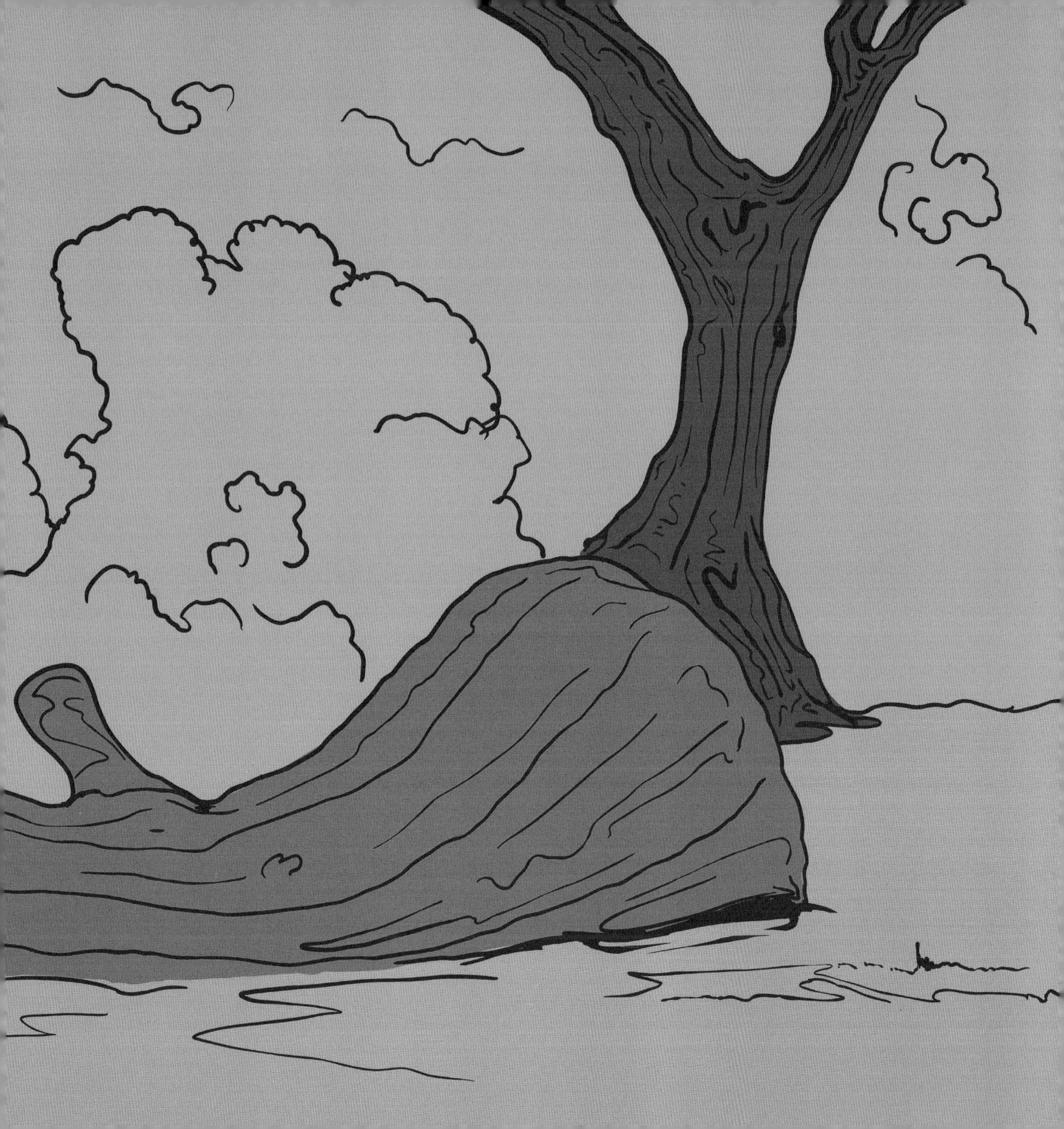

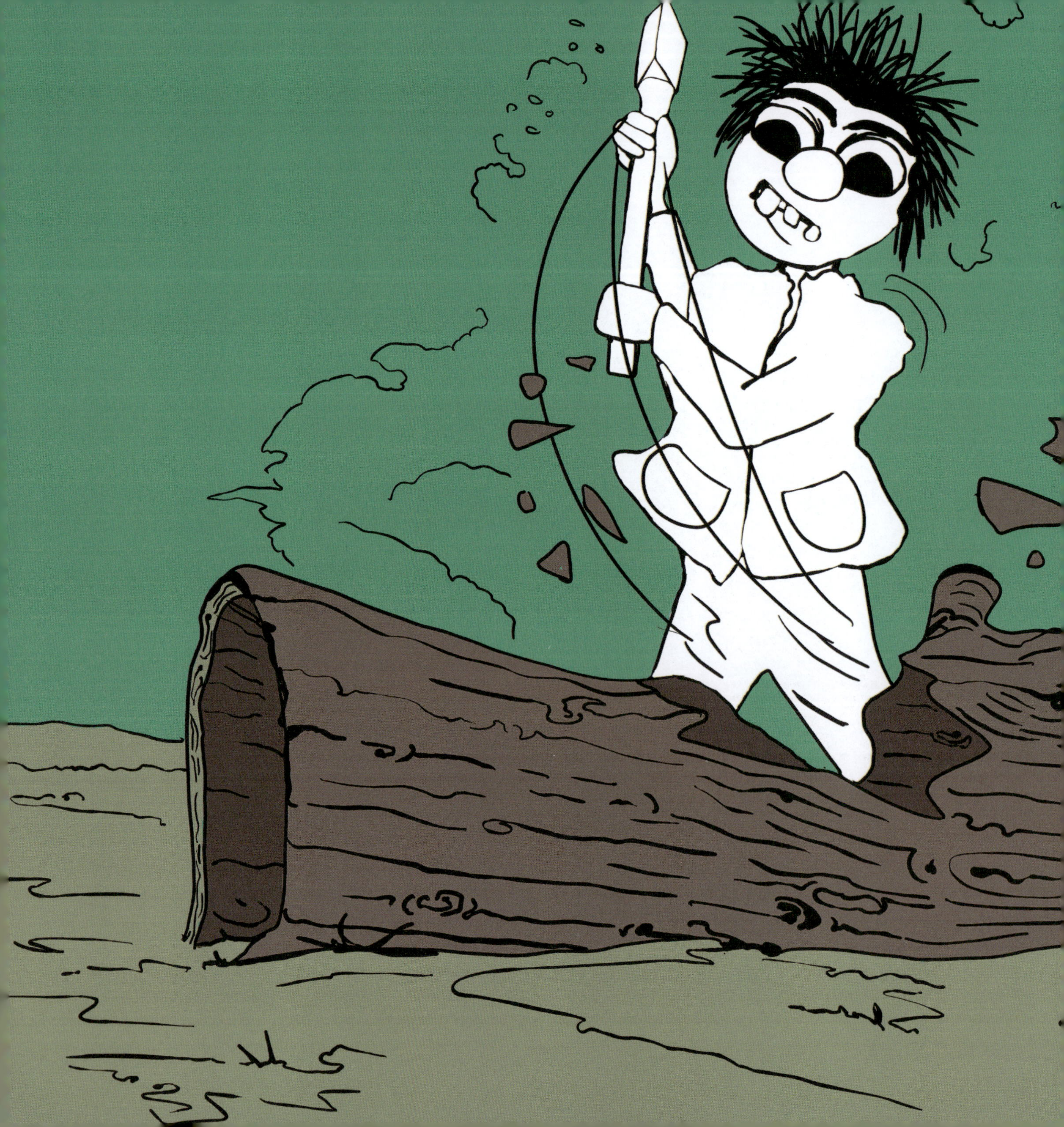

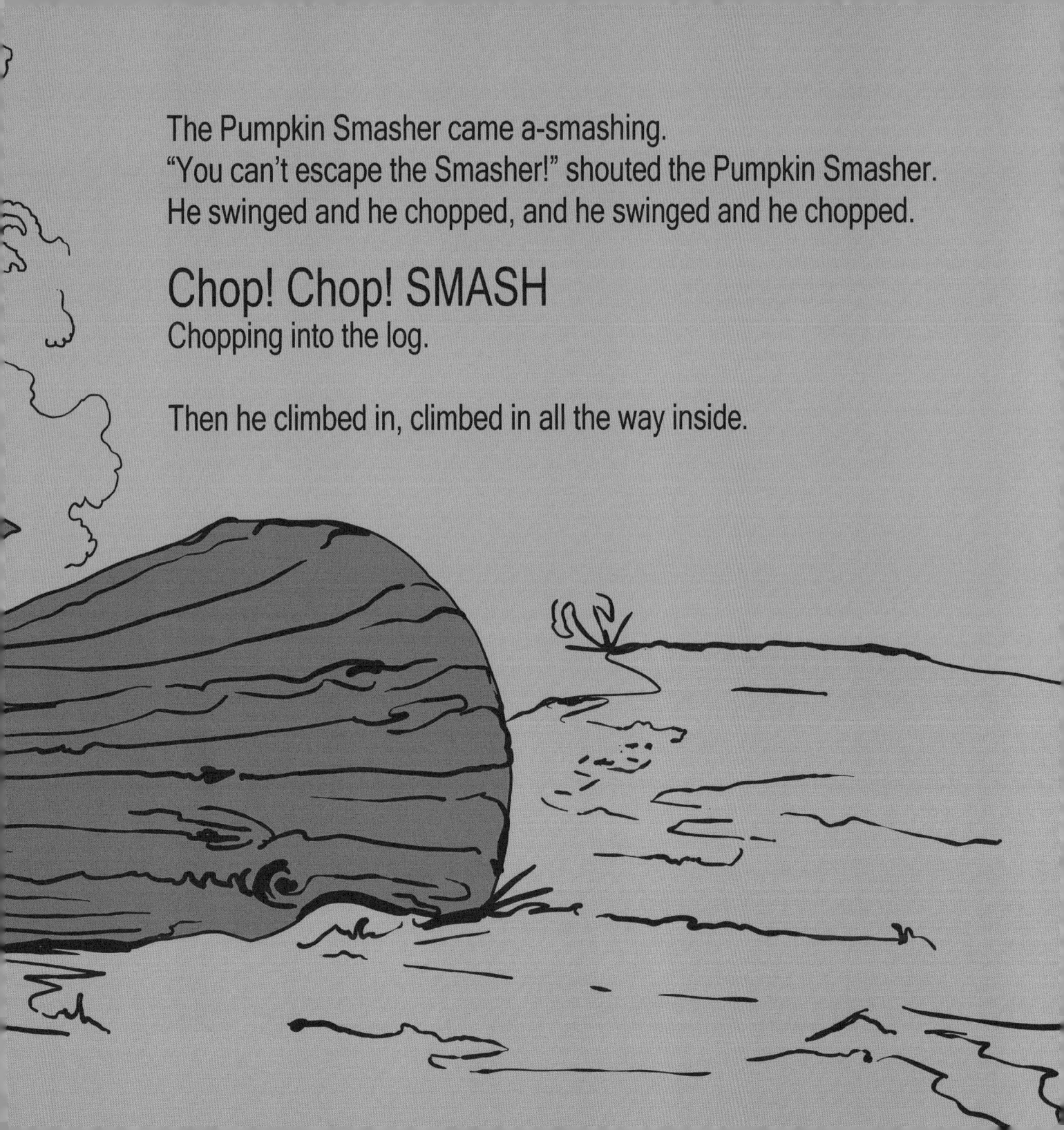

The Pumpkin Smasher came a-smashing.
"You can't escape the Smasher!" shouted the Pumpkin Smasher.
He swinged and he chopped, and he swinged and he chopped.

Chop! Chop! SMASH
Chopping into the log.

Then he climbed in, climbed in all the way inside.

John Pulp had carried on running down the inside.
He ran into the Underland where waiting,
beyond late, was a boat just for him.

"Climb aboard" said the Pumpkin Pie Man
"This is the last ride."

"It's OK, come back!"
said the Pumpkin Smasher
chasing behind, but he lied.
Swinging his axe
he had an axe to grind,
and was coming fast.

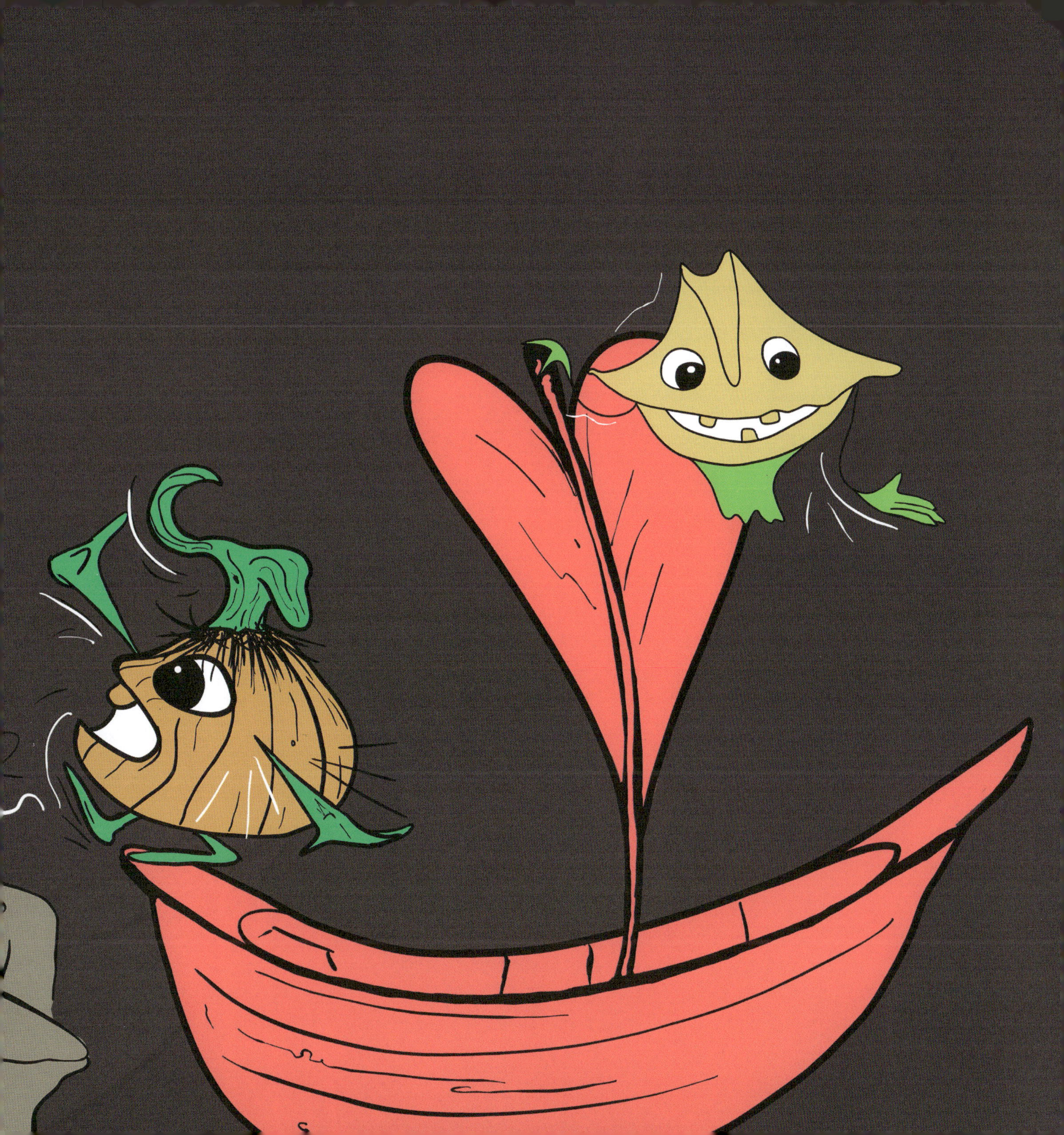

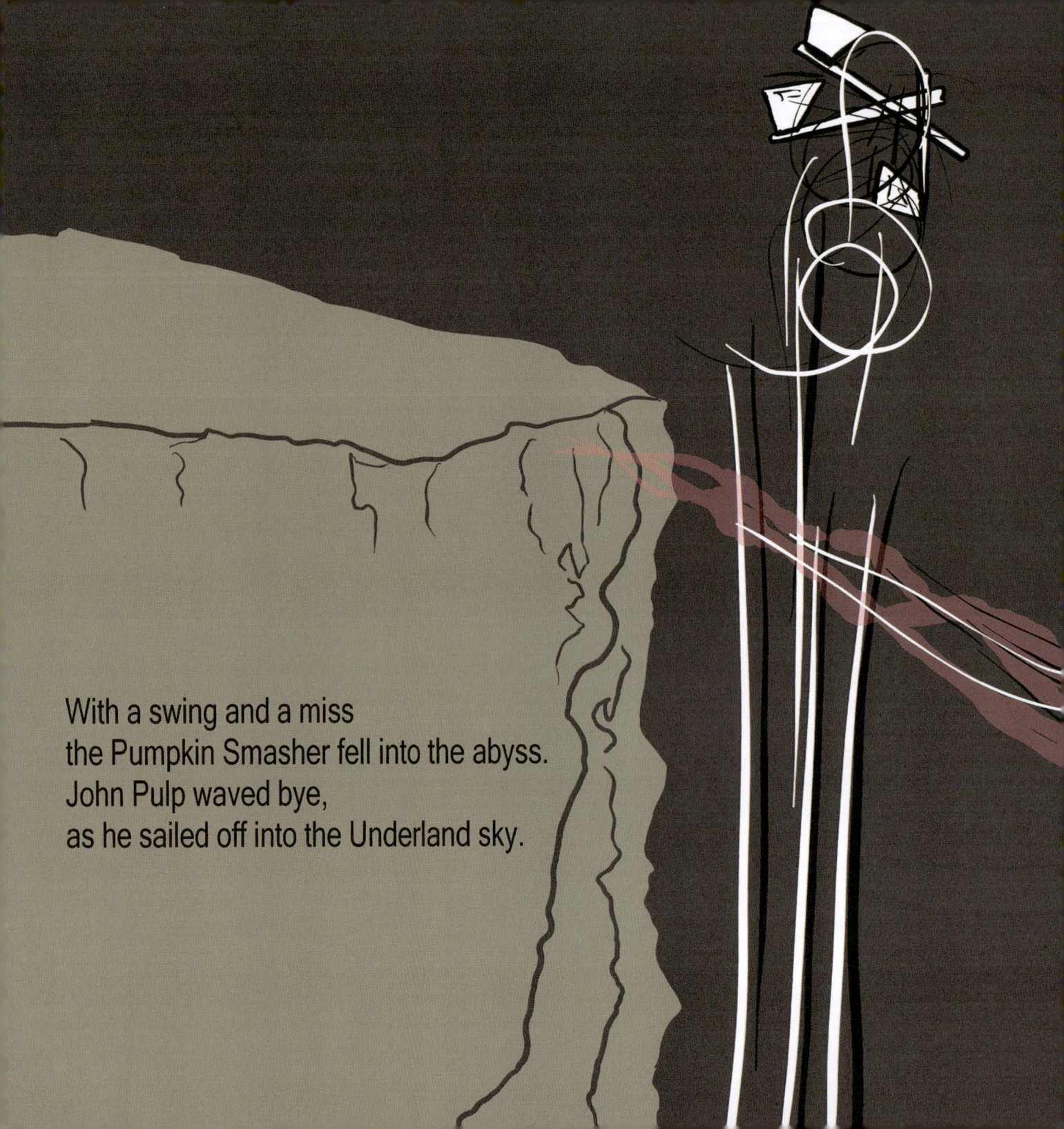

With a swing and a miss
the Pumpkin Smasher fell into the abyss.
John Pulp waved bye,
as he sailed off into the Underland sky.

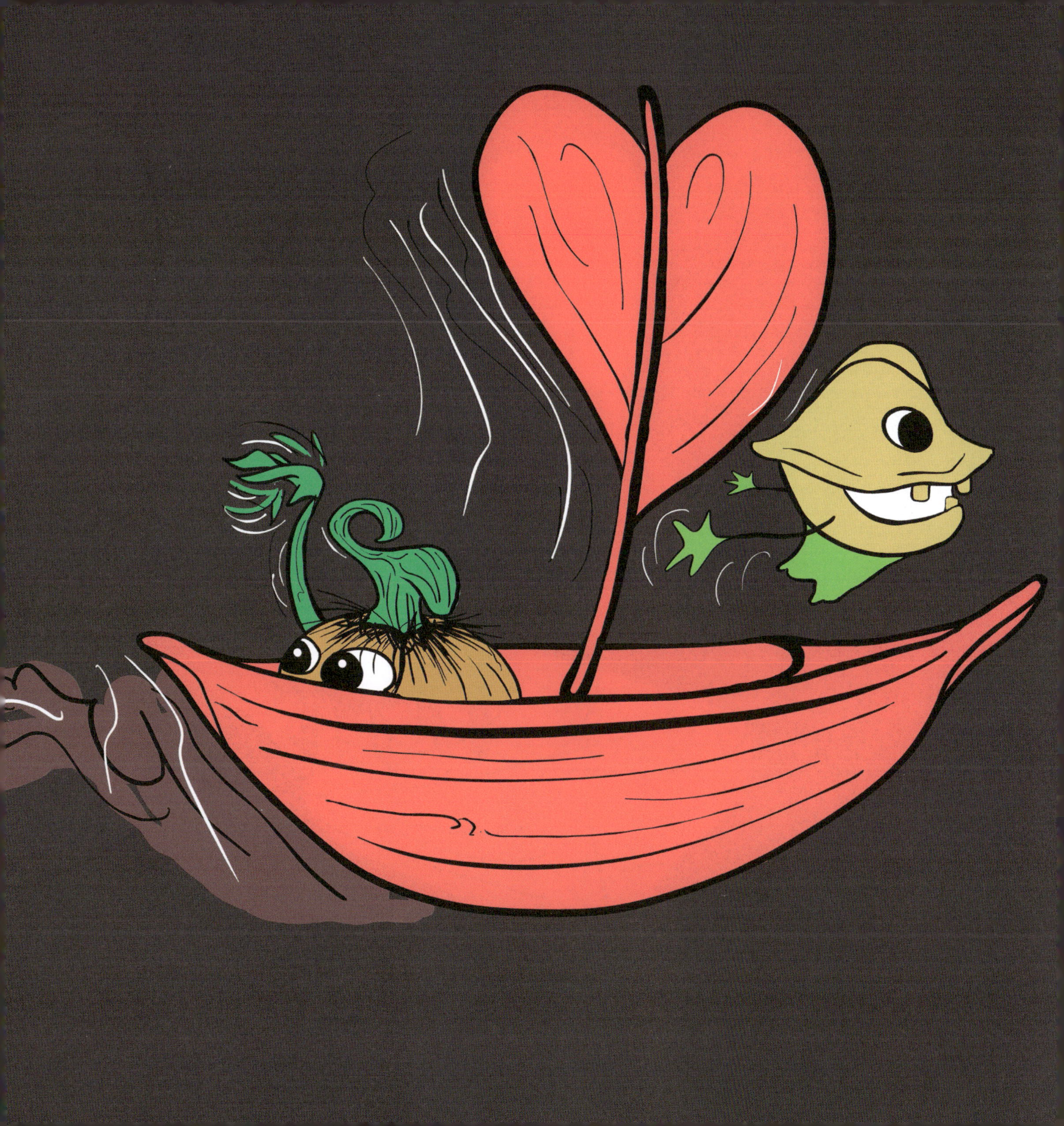

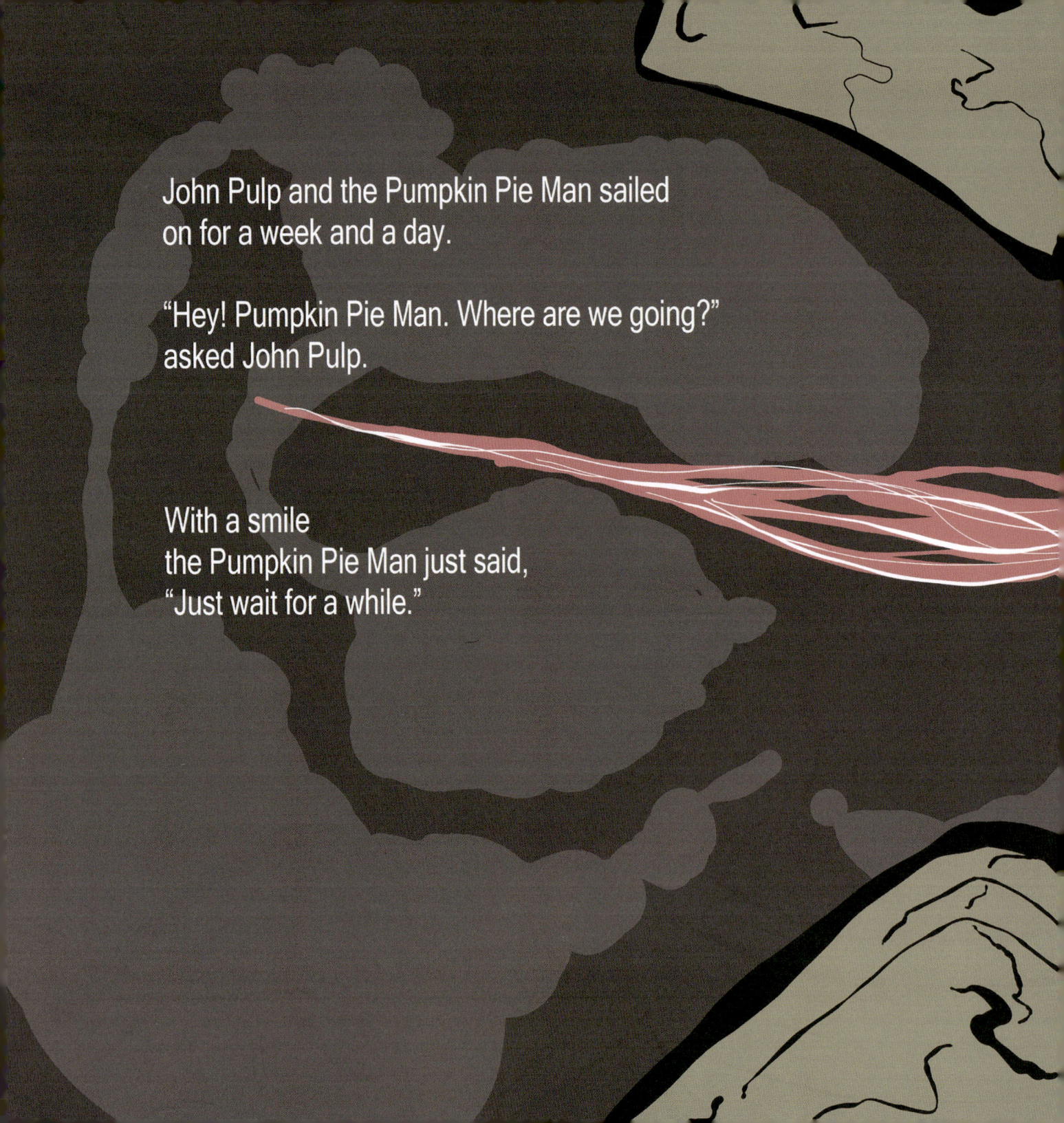

John Pulp and the Pumpkin Pie Man sailed
on for a week and a day.

"Hey! Pumpkin Pie Man. Where are we going?"
asked John Pulp.

With a smile
the Pumpkin Pie Man just said,
"Just wait for a while."

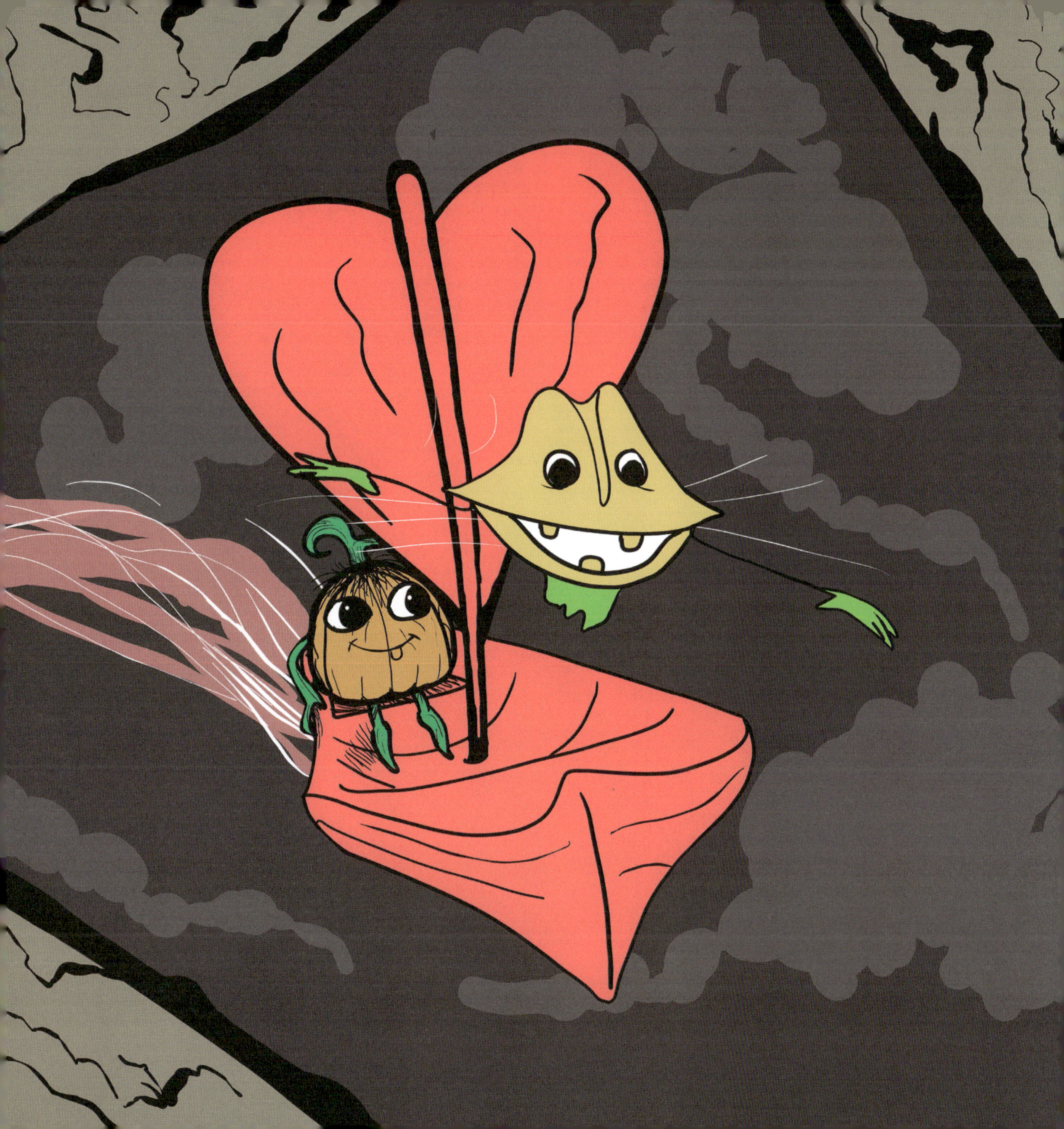

They came to a new land. A pumpkin land.

"Welcome to Pumpkinweenies Land!
A place under the Underland sky filled with joy."
said the king of the Pumpkinweenies,
greeting John Pulp personally.

And John Pulp was filled with joy.

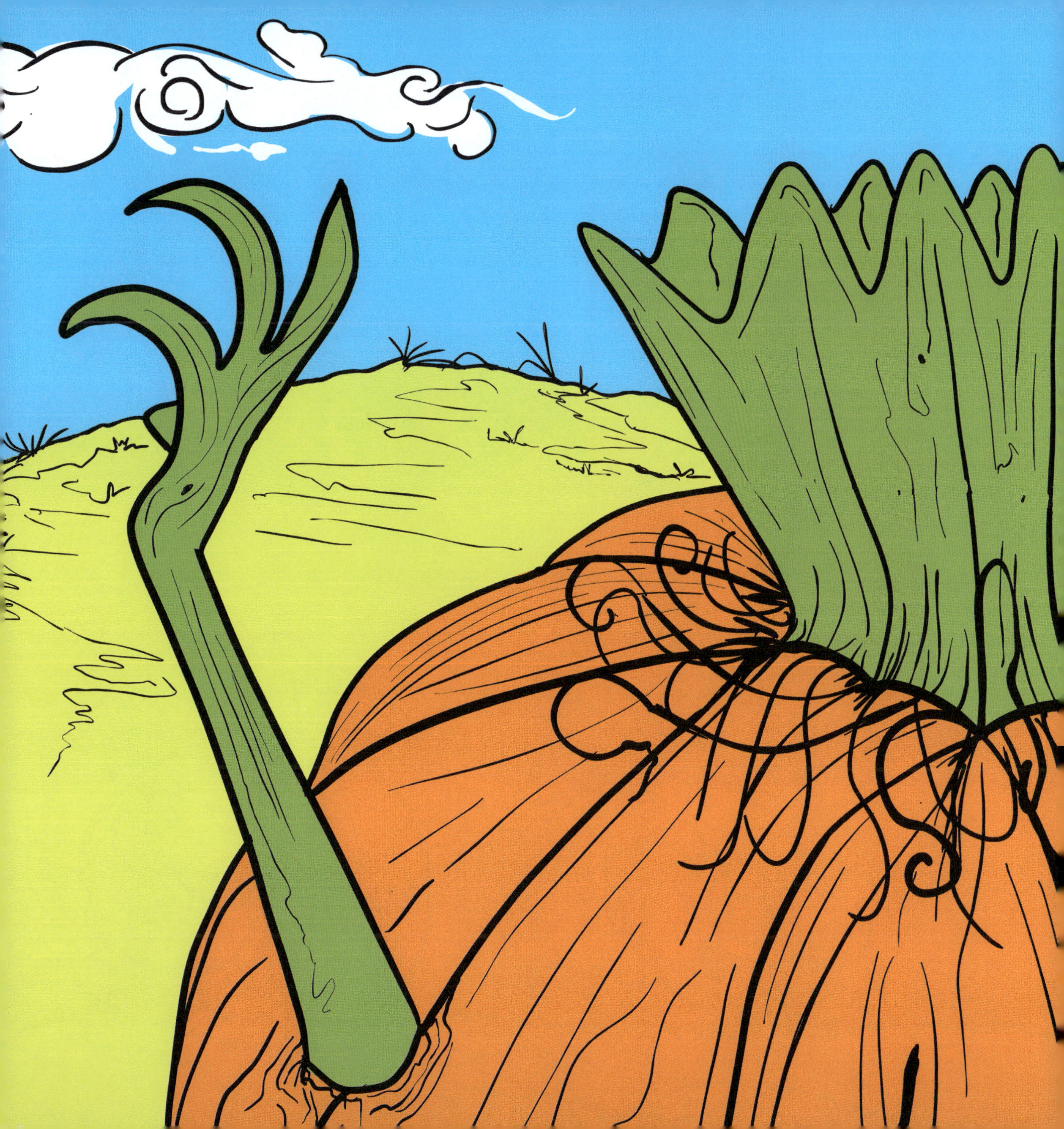

From near and far all Pumpkinweenies had come happily.

Here was a place,
a place to have fun
under the sun.

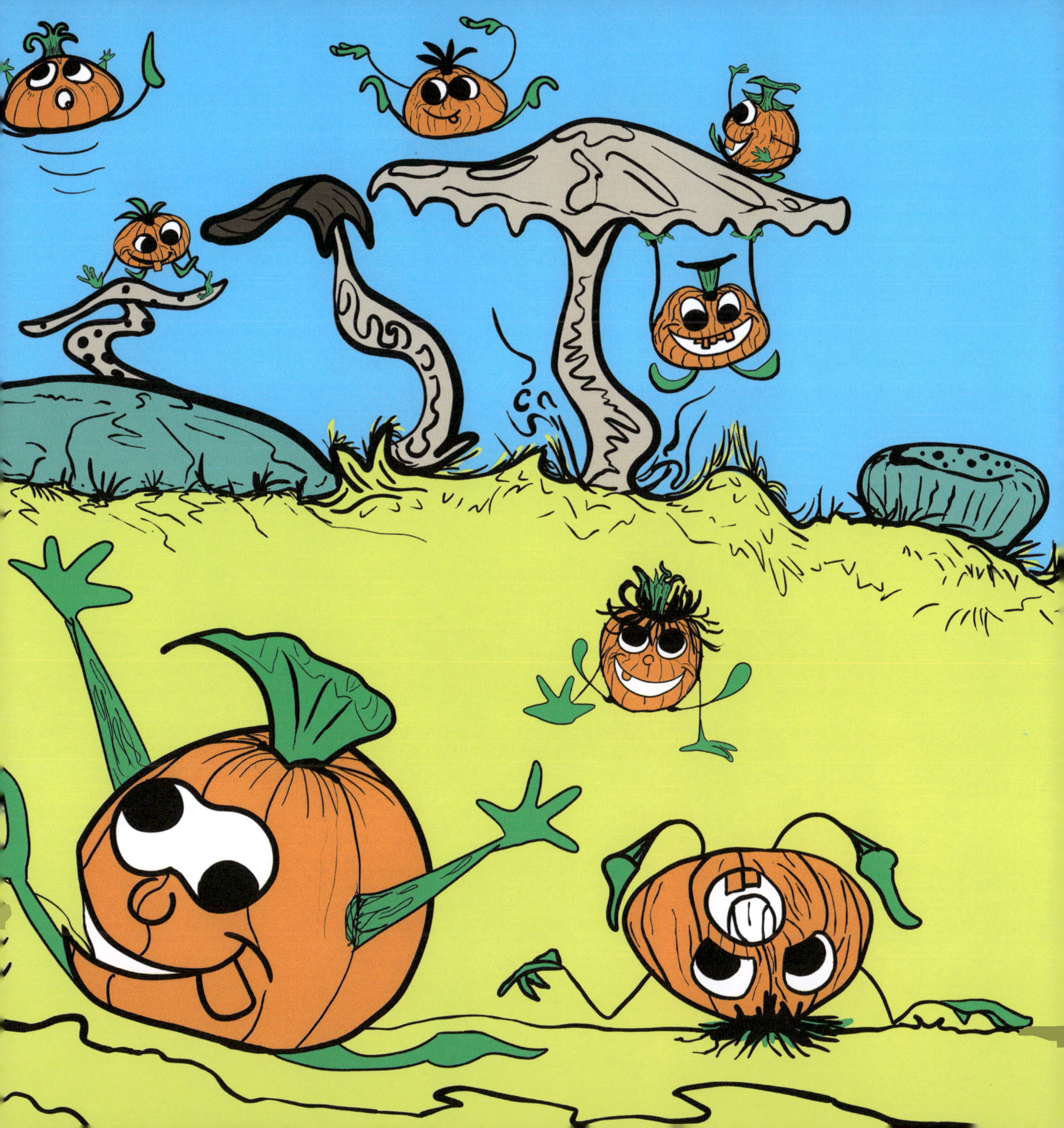

There were even Punpkinweenies having an egg and spoon race, laughing as they shouted, "This is ace!"

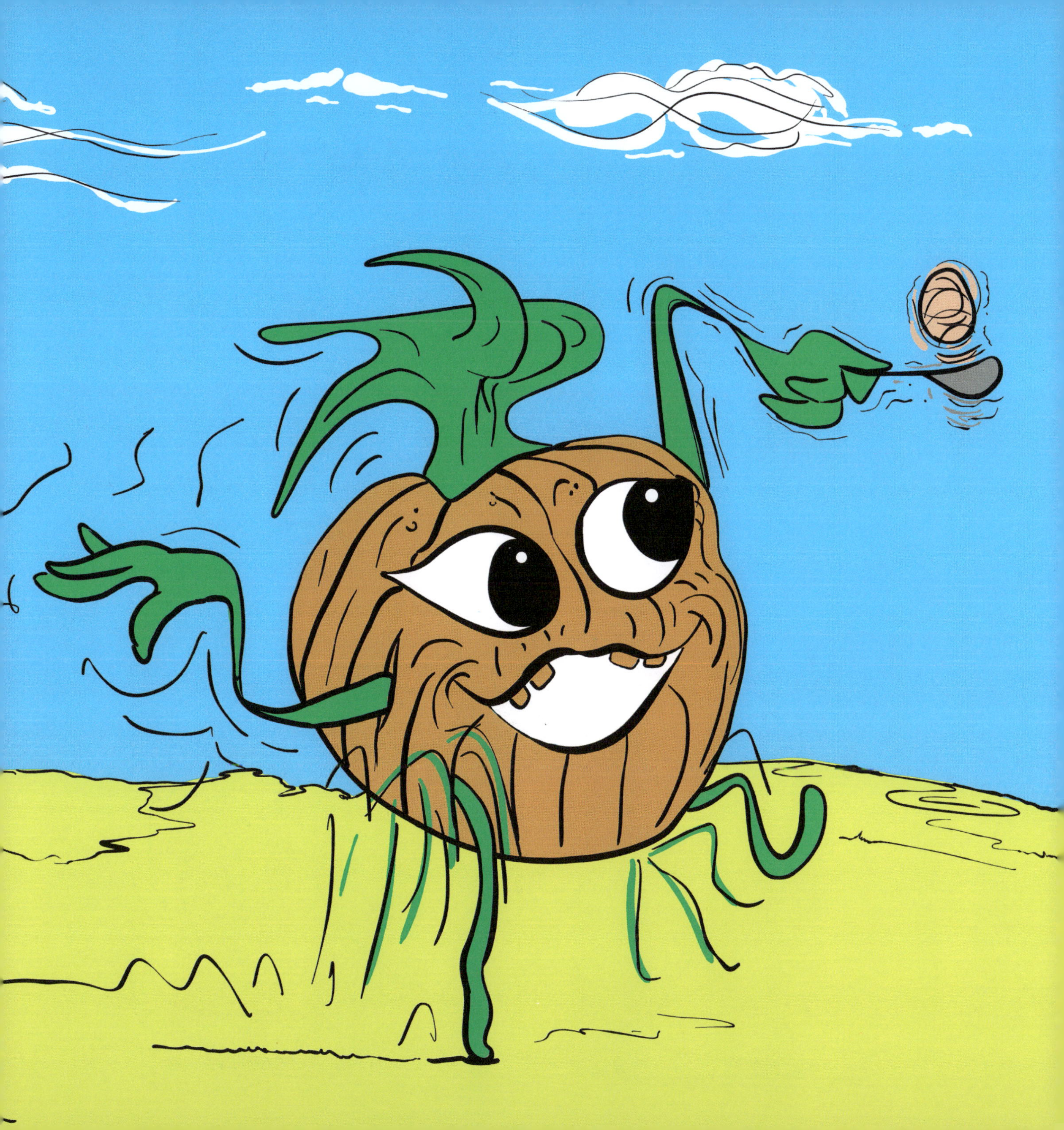

Then John Pulp made a friend.
She was Princess Pumpkin Twinkle.
She made his heart tinkle.
She was happy not cold,
and jolly and bold.

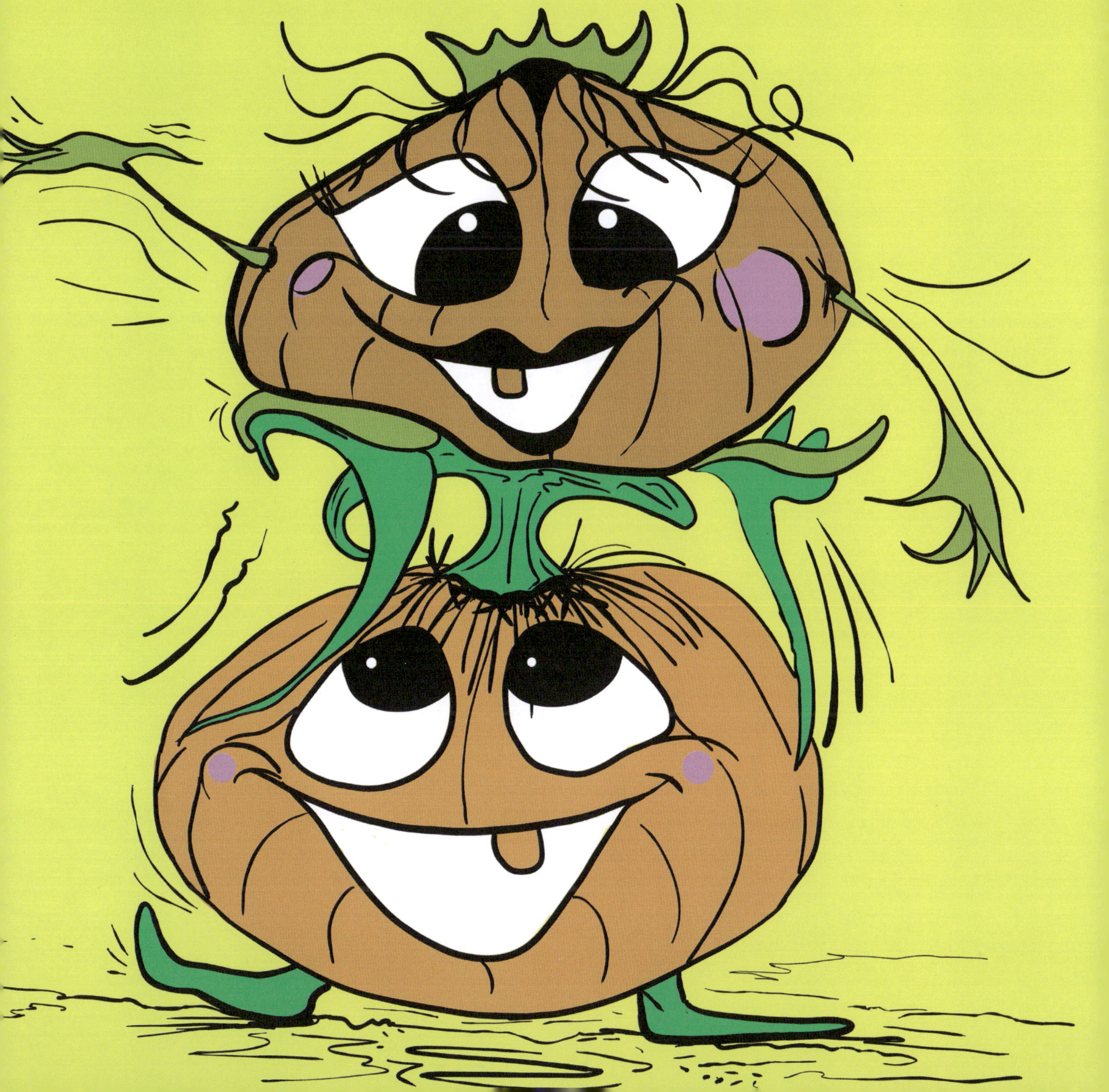

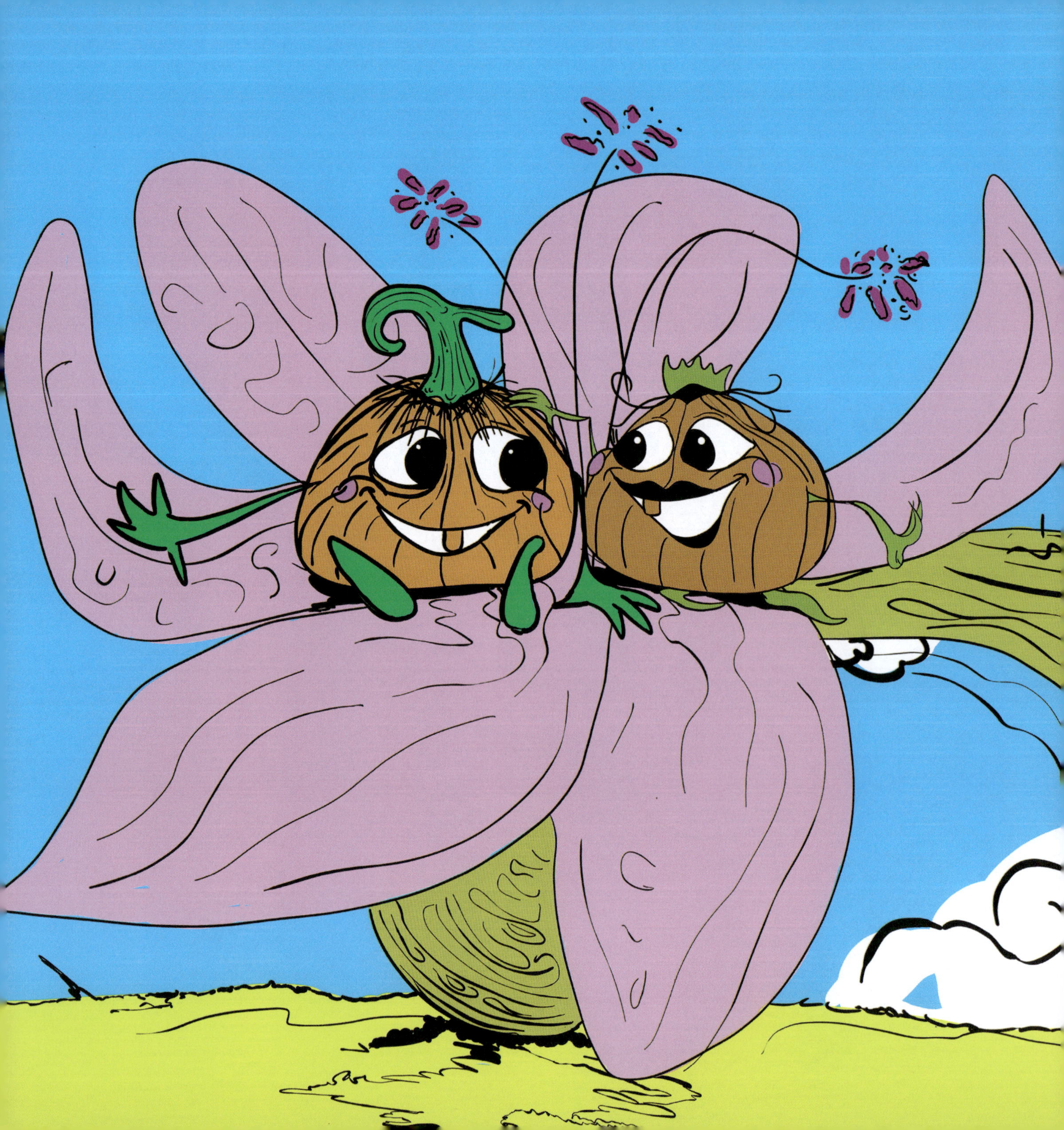

John Pulp had found his family.
He now lived in a flower, not up a tree.
Here they played all day long.
Never afraid but happy and family love strong.

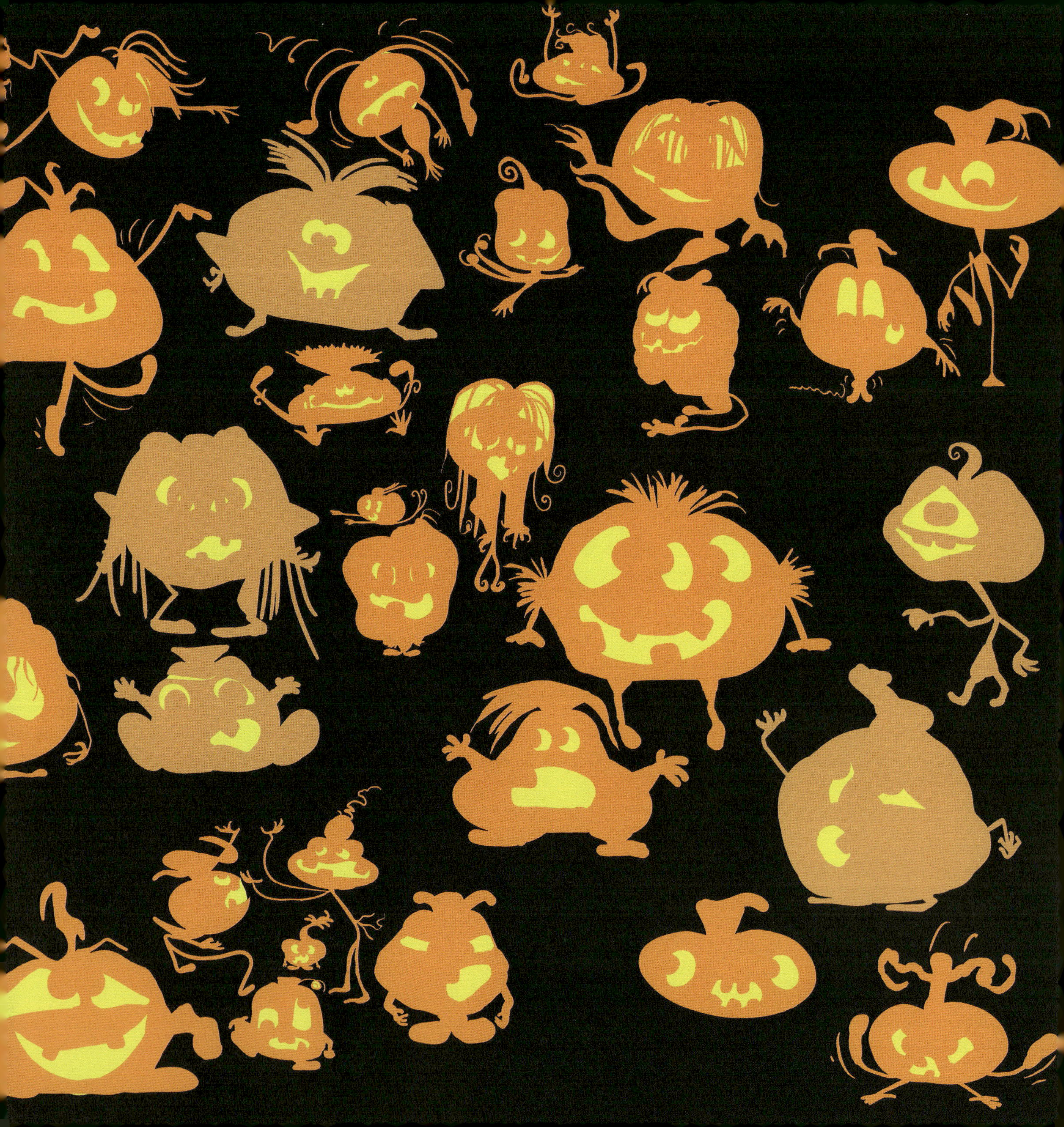

Printed in Great Britain
by Amazon